CLASSIC CAMERAS

CLASSIC CAMERAS

Kate Rouse

Eagle
Editions

A QUANTUM BOOK

Published by Eagle Editions Ltd
11 Heathfield
Royston
Hertfordshire SG8 5BW

Copyright ©MCMXCIV
Quintet Publishing Limited

This edition printed 2002

ISBN 1-86160-505-6

QUMFGC

This book is produced by
Quantum Publishing
6 Blundell Street
London N7 9BH

Printed in Singapore by
Star Standard Industries Pte Ltd

CONTENTS

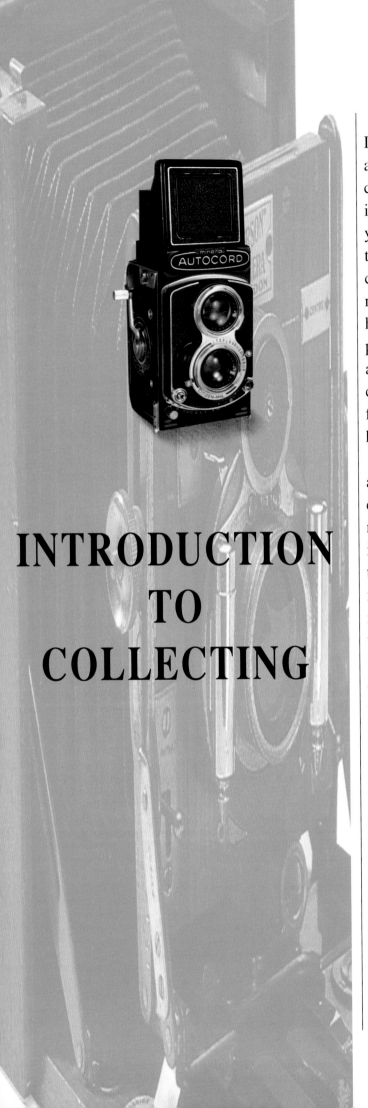

INTRODUCTION TO COLLECTING

WHAT TO COLLECT

In a book like this it is possible to cover only a tiny number of the cameras that are considered collectible but it is hoped that, by introducing you to just a few such cameras, you will want to go on and learn more about this intriguing hobby. Exactly what you choose to collect will depend partly on your motives. If you wish to collect purely for a hobby, then an interesting collection can be put together at modest prices using readily available cameras. However, if you prefer to collect as an investment, then a greater financial outlay will be needed and you will have to concentrate on the rarer cameras.

It is hard to define what 'collectible' means, as there are as many different types of collections as there are collectors; each person makes his or her own individual choice of items. However, as a rough guide to the first-time collector, any camera which is unusual or innovative for its time, or was the first to introduce some feature, is almost bound to be viewed as collectible in years to come.

Collectors usually start with a general collection with no particular direction, but they frequently move on to concentrate on just one theme. For instance, this could be one manufacturer, such as Leica; or one period, such as the last century; or one type of camera, such as 35mm. The ideas are endless. These thematic collections typically contain not only the cameras, but also all sorts of associated accessories, advertisements, literature, etc., which bring the collection to life.

HOW TO COLLECT

Old cameras are available from many different sources. There are stores specializing in selling them and auction houses often include

them in collectors' sales. Bargains can sometimes be found by keeping an eye on advertisements for second-hand goods in magazines and newspapers, and local camera shops frequently sell second-hand cameras which are of interest to the collector.

Collectors' clubs organize fairs where cameras can be bought and sold, and where you can meet fellow enthusiasts to exchange ideas and information. These clubs are a great help to the beginner and a list of the major ones can be found in the appendix.

WHAT ABOUT THE PRICE?

This is always a question which worries the first-time collector - is the price right? There is no easy answer but luckily there are sources of help. Perhaps the best known of these is *McKeown's Price Guide to Antique and Classic Cameras*, published in America by Centennial Photo. This book is produced every two years and lists over 8000 cameras, with notes on how to identify each model and the range of prices that it might fetch on the worldwide markets.

It is important to remember when looking at a camera to take into account its condition. The prices quoted in price guides like McKeown's are for 'average' condition - that is in working order and showing a few signs of normal use, but not too damaged. If a camera is in mint condition, boxed with instructions, it may fetch twice the listed price; if it is in very poor condition, it may be worth only a quarter of the price, or less.

LOOKING AFTER A COLLECTION

To enjoy your collection you will want to bring the best out of each camera by keeping it in good condition. In many cases, this can be done very quickly and easily.

When cleaning a camera it is important to use materials which will not harm it. Modern cleaners frequently contain chemicals which are potentially damaging; for example, the lens cleaning fluid sold for modern cameras can dissolve the cement used to hold old lenses in place. It is therefore important to use traditional cleaning methods. For wood this means linseed oil to prevent drying and beeswax furniture polish to give a good sheen. For leather, use a mixture of lanolin and beeswax (sold as 'hide feed' or 'leather-bound book polish'). Shoe polish can be used to remove scuff marks. Metal parts should be cleaned with a non-abrasive cleaner without a solvent, which could remove the varnish that covers the brass used on cameras from the last century. A mixture of ten parts water to one part vinegar works well in most cases.

Lenses are made of very soft glass which scratches easily. Special blower brushes and tissues are available from photographic shops and these must be used in preference to any other cloth or tissue. First remove any visible dust with the brush, then breathe on the lens and clean while still moist with a circular motion of the tissue.

In the case of badly worn or damaged cameras, it may be best to ask a specialist to repair the camera. There are a few people who specialize in restoring antique cameras; they can be found through books and collectors' clubs.

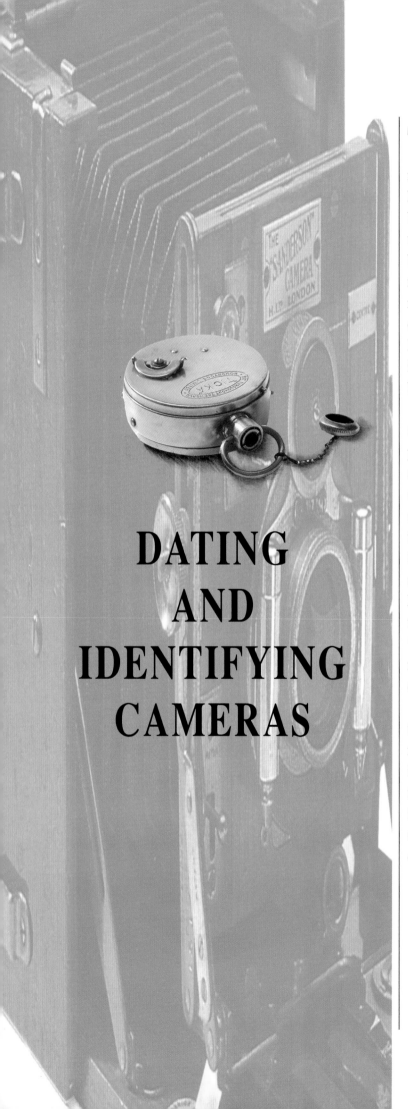

DATING AND IDENTIFYING CAMERAS

There are several useful pointers to use when faced with an unknown camera, but each must be used with care, as later repairs might have altered the original camera. For example, the bellows on cameras were generally red in colour up to 1900 and were then gradually replaced with black ones. However, since the bellows are the most fragile part of such cameras, they frequently needed repairing, and many cameras which originally had red bellows now have black ones. Hence a camera from the last century could be incorrectly dated as post-1900 if the colour of the bellows were used as the only evidence.

Also, a lens is not necessarily the original one sold with the camera. They were often replaced by photographers who, for various reasons, preferred a different lens to the one supplied. Likewise, shutters may not be original, as they used to be sold as separate accessories and not, like many of today's shutters, as an integral part of the camera. Some popular manufacturers of shutters from around the turn of the century, such as Thornton-Pickard, sold their shutters to other manufacturers to be put on to their cameras. Hence if the name 'Thornton-Pickard' appears on the shutter, it does not imply that they necessarily made the entire camera.

So dating an unknown camera is best done by taking several factors into account and not by relying upon just one feature. These factors include camera type, lens, shutter, camera body features, patent numbers and serial numbers. The information in the following reference tables should be useful when dating an unknown camera:

LENS TYPES:

Lenses often have written on them a name or design type and these can be used to date the lens. The years of introduction of some of the more common types of lenses are:

Anastigmat	1890
Aplanat	1866
Cooke Triplet	1893
Dagor (name variant of Goerz Double Anastigmat)	1904
Goerz Double Anastigmat	1892
Heliar	1900
Petzval Portrait lens	1840
Planar	1896
Protar (name variant of Zeiss Anastigmat)	1900
Rapid Rectilinear	1866
Tessar	1902
Telephoto	1891
Unar	1899
Xpres	1913

Between 1858 and the late 1880s, most lenses used a set of brass diaphragms called Waterhouse stops, which were inserted into a slot in the lens mount. From 1887, iris diaphragms began to be used commercially, although earlier lenses may have been adapted for their use.

The first commercial use of lens coating to reduce reflections occurred in 1936 and by the 1950s the technique was being extensively used. In early examples, look for a red letter 'C' or a small red triangle on the lens to indicate that it is coated.

SHUTTER TYPES:

Although earlier examples of shutters exist, they did not come into regular use until the 1880s when photographic plates were becoming too fast to be used without one. The years of introduction of some of the more common types of shutter are:

Actus	1912
Automat	1901
Compound	1903
Compur - Dial set	1912
Compur - Rim set	1928
Compur Rapid	1935
Dakon	1940
Focal-Plane Shutters - came into common use	1890s
Kodak Ball Bearing	1909
Kodex	1924
Koilos	1904
Prontor S	1948
Synchro Compur	1951
Thornton-Pickard Time and Instantaneous	1892
Unicum	1897
Victo A	1914
Victo B	1918
Victor	1894

CAMERA BODY FEATURES:

Since both shutters and lenses could be, and frequently were, changed, they provide a somewhat unreliable source for dating. Features on the camera body itself are usually more reliable, with the exception of the bellows (as mentioned above) and the back (which could be replaced on certain cameras to take different types of film or plates).

AUTOGRAPHIC FEATURE Only used on Kodak cameras between 1914 and 1932. However, some earlier models of Kodaks were adapted by buying a special Autographic back, so this feature must be used with care when dating Kodak cameras. See page 30 for details of the different designs of this feature.

BELLOWS Red or maroon coloured until c1900 when black ones were introduced. Over the next ten years, black ones gradually replaced red ones. Until 1890s, bellows had square corners, but after that time they were chamfered to reduce damage.

BODY SHUTTER RELEASE Folding rollfilm cameras changed from having the shutter release on the shutter itself to having it placed more conveniently on the camera body in the early 1930s.

COUPLED RANGEFINDERS Introduced by Kodak in 1916, but other manufacturers did not follow their lead until the 1930s.

LEATHER COVERING From the early 1890s onwards.

METAL PARTS
brass Mostly pre- 1910.
aluminium Late 1890s onwards.
nickel-plating Late 1890s onwards. This type of plating always looks shiny and just slightly yellow.

chromium-plating Mid-1930s onwards. Brighter than nickel-plating, with no hint of yellow. Although sometimes shiny, chromium-plating can also have a matt finish.
sheet metal Camera parts were cut out of sheet metal up to the First World War, when casting took over as a quicker and cheaper alternative.
casting Used from c1905 onwards, it gradually took over as one of the main ways to construct a camera body and all of its parts. The improved die casting was introduced in the late 1930s.

PLASTIC CAMERAS Although Kodak used a little bakelite for some camera parts around the First World War, it was not until the 1930s that plastics became extensively used.

RED WINDOW IN CAMERA BACK Used with rollfilm to see which number on the film had been reached, this useful feature was first used in 1892. A second window in the camera back may be found from 1922 onwards.

SELF-ERECTING FRONT This feature on folding rollfilm cameras allowed the lens to assume its correct position automatically as the camera was opened. It was rare before the mid-1920s, but then took over as the standard design.

WOODEN CAMERAS Dovetail jointing up to the turn of the century, then machined comb joints. Wet plate cameras of 1850s-1870s may show blackish silver nitrate stains around the plate holder.

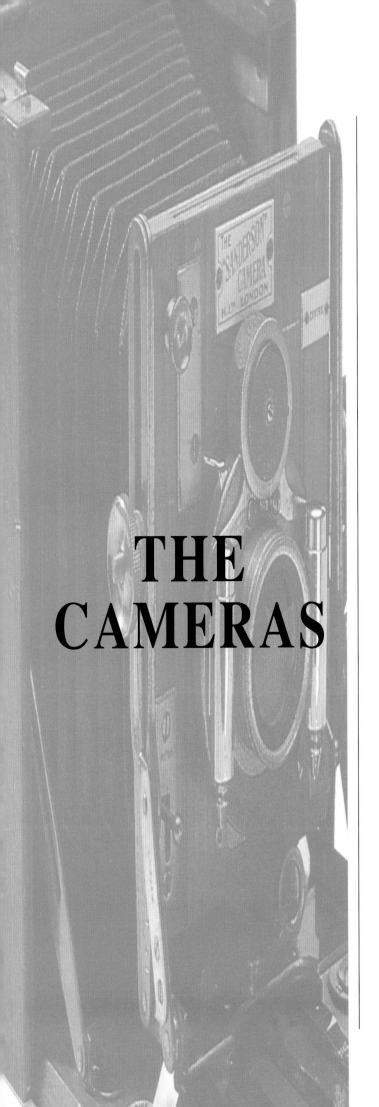

THE
CAMERAS

Early Plate Cameras

(1840s-*c*.1890s)

CHAPTER 1

THE EARLY YEARS

It is one of the many intriguing things about the history of photography that 'cameras' existed before photography had been invented. For several centuries artists had used an instrument called a portable camera obscura to help them to draw scenes accurately, and this device was the forerunner of photographic cameras.

In 1839, the Frenchman Louis Daguerre and the Englishman William Henry Fox Talbot both

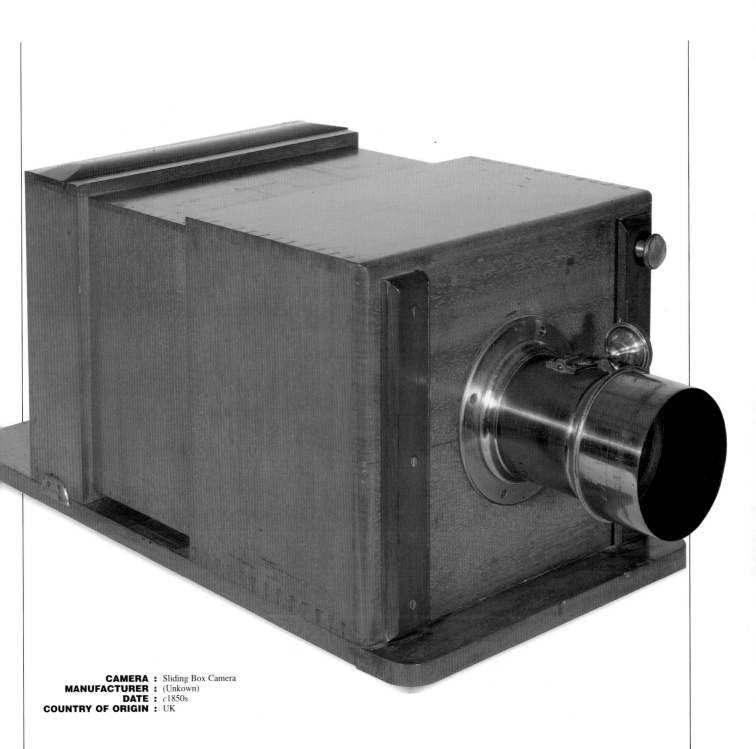

CAMERA : Sliding Box Camera
MANUFACTURER : (Unkown)
DATE : *c*1850s
COUNTRY OF ORIGIN : UK

announced that they had found ways of recording an image by the action of light on certain silver-based chemicals - photography had been born. After his announcement, Daguerre quickly set about designing a camera for use with his new process. Manufactured by Alphonse Giroux et Cie in Paris, it was the first commercially produced photographic camera. It used plates of the size 16.5 x 21.5cm (6½ x 8½ inches), which became known as 'whole-plate size' and was a standard in

photography for more than a century.

Daguerre's design was based on one which had been used for artists' camera obscuras in the 1700s. It is called the 'sliding box' design and was frequently used for early photographic cameras. The illustration on the opposite page shows this design, which is made of two rigid wooden boxes, one inside the other. The inner box slides in and out to focus the picture.

Clearly this design was somewhat cumbersome

and it was not long before camera manufacturers started to look for some means of producing a folding camera which would be more portable. The introduction of the first glass negatives in 1851 gave a further incentive to make cameras less bulky. Since these 'wet plates' needed immediate processing, the photographer had to carry a portable darkroom around as well as the camera!

Throughout the 1850s, manufacturers turned increasingly to the use of leather bellows as a means of making a camera more compact. The first bellows used were parallel-sided, but in 1856 a Scotsman, C.G.H. Kinnear, designed a camera with tapered bellows. These could concertina into a considerably smaller size, since each fold of leather fitted inside the next, larger fold. It is a design of bellows which is still being used today on large-format field cameras.

CAMERA : Wet Plate Camera
MANUFACTURER : Oscar Kramer
DATE : *c*1860s
COUNTRY OF ORIGIN : Austria

DRY PLATE CAMERAS

When wet plates were finally superseded in the late 1870s by dry plates, which did not require a portable darkroom, the basic camera designs continued for a while along similar lines. With the exception of cameras designed solely for use in the studio, the important thing was to have a camera which could fold into a convenient size for carrying. Two major designs emerged and are illustrated here.

The Instanto camera, made in England by E. & T. Underwood, is of the 'tailboard' design, where the hinged wooden baseboard at the back of the camera folds up over the glass focusing screen. When the camera was in use, this tailboard dropped down to act as the base along which the back could be moved for focusing. The Meagher camera is also of this design but with an extra piece of wood at the side to give better protection to the bellows and added rigidity.

The other camera by E. & T. Underwood illustrated here is of the alternative 'front-folding' design, where the hinged baseboard folded up over the lens panel. Some cameras of this design had a hole in the board to let the lens through, but with others it was necessary to remove the lens before folding the camera.

There were many minor variations on the designs above, such as the field cameras made in the 1880s by the American company Scovill. These were essentially a combination of the two designs above, since the baseboard was hinged at both the rear and the front of the camera, with the bellows capable of extending in both directions.

The identification of plate cameras from the first fifty years of photography can be problematical since manufacturers frequently did not put their names on them. Many good examples exist on the collectors' market at quite reasonable prices with absolutely no identifying marks on either the camera or its lens. To make matters even more confusing, when a name does appear it may be that of the company which sold the camera and not of the manufacturer, who was often making cameras for several retail outlets. A few useful hints on how to date some of these early cameras are given on page 11.

CAMERA : Tailboard Plate Camera
MANUFACTURER : P. Meagher
DATE : c1880
COUNTRY OF ORIGIN : UK

CAMERA : The Instanto
MANUFACTURER : E. & T. Underwood
DATE : c1890-c1904
COUNTRY OF ORIGIN : UK

CAMERA : The Tourograph
MANUFACTURER : E. & T. Underwood
DATE : c1897
COUNTRY OF ORIGIN : UK

LATER PLATE CAMERAS

(*c*1890S ONWARDS)

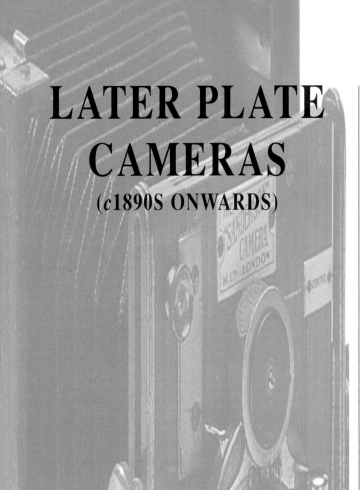

Hand Cameras

The rise of dry plates from the late 1870s onwards, and the introduction of rollfilm a decade later, widened the appeal of photography. Before these inventions appeared, photographers had to know enough chemistry to prepare and process their own plates, but now plates and film could be purchased ready-made and processed by someone else. Inevitably, with this explosion of interest came a mass of new cameras, and fierce competition between the manufacturers. If photography in its first fifty years was represented mainly by anonymous cameras, it was subsequently to become dominated by individual manufacturers.

With the general public becoming increasingly involved in photography, there was a demand for cameras of convenient size for taking snapshots.

CHAPTER 2

CAMERA : Sanderson Tropical Field Camera
MANUFACTURER : G. Houghton & Sons
DATE : *c*1905-1920s
COUNTRY OF ORIGIN : UK

CAMERA : Pony Premo No.4
MANUFACTURER : Rochester Optical Co.
DATE : *c*1900-1912
COUNTRY OF ORIGIN : USA

CAMERA : Pocket Wizard I
MANUFACTURER : Manhattan Optical Co.
DATE : Late 1890s
COUNTRY OF ORIGIN : USA

Hence the earlier 'stand' cameras, so-called because they needed a tripod or stand, were gradually joined by 'hand' cameras which could be hand held. Two typical American hand cameras are shown here - the Pocket Wizard I and the Pony Premo No. 4.

The Wizard cameras were made from the mid-1890s by the Manhattan Optical Company, in several models and sizes from quarter-plate, which measures 8.2 x 10.8cm (3¼ x 4¼ inches), to 12.7 x 17.8cm (5 x 7 inches). The Pony Premo No. 4 was made by the Rochester Optical Co. around the turn of the century and again was one of a series of similar models which remained in production even after the company had been taken over by Eastman Kodak in 1903.

Both cameras show two additions to the early plate cameras dealt with in the last chapter - a viewfinder and a shutter. Although shutters had been around for a considerable time, they had been an accessory rather than a necessity, but the new dry plates were generally too fast to be used without one, so they became a standard part of a camera's design.

In 1895 the Englishman Frederick H. Sanderson patented a mechanism for swinging the front lens panel (camera movements of this type are highly useful to the photographer in a variety of circumstances). Initially, the Sanderson camera was made as an ordinary stand camera, but in 1899 a hand version was brought out. Two models are shown here, one is the usual leather covered version, the other is a so-called 'tropical' model.

Tropical cameras were made specifically for use in hot climates, using wood which was less likely to warp (teak in this case) and extra metal bracing to stop such warping. The bellows were usually made of cloth, not leather, since certain tropical insects and moulds are fond of attacking leather!

Many of the hand cameras looked like smaller

versions of the front-folding plate cameras from earlier in the century with the addition of the shutter and viewfinder. However, two other designs were popular - folding strut cameras, which used struts to support the lens panel, and box cameras (which are covered later in the chapter).

A well-known camera of the strut design was the Anschütz made by C. P. Goerz of Berlin. It was named after its designer, Ottomar Anschütz, who had developd the shutter used in the camera specially for his pioneering action photography. It was a focal-plane shutter made of fabric and capable of speeds as fast as 1/1000 second. The first model (1890) had a rigid body, but in 1896 the folding strut version appeared. It influenced

the design of cameras for press photographers for many years, particularly in continental Europe.

The Klapp camera made by Heinrich Ernemann of Dresden, Germany, was another example of the strut design. It was long-lived, with several models produced between 1904 and 1926. This period also covers some important developments in the German photographic industry, which was to be one of the leading photographic industries during the first half of this century. The smaller companies began to amalgamate into large organizations, finally culminating in the formation of Zeiss Ikon AG in 1926.

As companies combined, the production of a given series of cameras often continued under the new company name. This can be seen with the

CAMERA : Sanderson Regulai
MANUFACTURER : G. Houghton & Sons
DATE : *c*1903-1920s
COUNTRY OF ORIGIN : UK

models of the Ideal camera which was first manufactured c1907 by R. Hüttig & Sohn in Dresden. In 1909 Hüttig was the senior partner in an amalgamation of four companies to form Ica AG which, in turn, formed part of the giant Zeiss Ikon in 1926. During the 1920s Ica produced several models of a camera called the Ideal, whose design is clearly developed from Hüttig's original. Production of the Ideal camera continued into the late 1930s under the Zeiss Ikon banner.

A few German camera manufacturers retained their independence and one of the best known is

V. Linhof of Munich. Their folding plate cameras initially appeared just before the First World War and led to a succession of Linhof cameras which were renowned for their fine workmanship. The prices of their later cameras tend to be determined more by the fact that they are still usable than by the collectors' market.

One problem with the early plate cameras was that the plates could only be loaded one at a time. To take more than one picture entailed carrying a bag full of unexposed plates loaded into their holders, called dark slides. With the introduction

CAMERA : Ideal
MANUFACTURER : Zeiss Ikon
DATE : 1926-1938
COUNTRY OF ORIGIN : Germany

CAMERA : Klapp Tropical model
MANUFACTURER : H. Ernemann
DATE : 1904-1926
COUNTRY OF ORIGIN : Germany

CAMERA : Anschütz (strut-type)
MANUFACTURER : C. P. Goerz
DATE : 1896-1910
COUNTRY OF ORIGIN : Germany

of rollfilm in the late 1880s, this restriction in the design of plate cameras was made all the more apparent. To counter this, manufacturers began to look for ways of holding more than one plate at a time inside the camera. The simple box design of plate cameras had become increasingly popular during the 1880s, and lent itself to use for this purpose.

The simplest way to carry extra plates was to have a storage area built into the camera body. The Kodak Eureka of 1897-1899 used this principle to carry three double dark slides (six plates). Another technique is shown in the camera of the same name (but no relation) patented by the British manufacturer W. W. Rouch in 1887. It had a magazine holding twelve plates with a light-tight bag situated over its open top. After each exposure, the photographer could lift a plate up into the bag using a lever and then manipulate it to the other side of the pack by hand.

A popular design of the 1890s and early 1900s was the falling-plate camera. The pack of plates was held against a stop by a spring and, after the front one had been exposed, the stop could be released using a catch to allow the plate to drop into the bottom of the camera. The action of the spring then moved the pack along so that the second plate now lay against the stop ready for exposure. The Klito camera made by Houghton's during the first two decades of this century was a very popular British example of this design.

An unusual design was marketed by the English firm J. Fallowfield in their Facile camera. The plates were held in two

CAMERA :	No. 2 Bullet
MANUFACTURER :	Eastman Kodak
DATE :	1895-1900
COUNTRY OF ORIGIN :	USA

CAMERA :	Eureka
MANUFACTURER :	W. W. Rouch & Co.
DATE :	1887
COUNTRY OF ORIGIN :	UK

slotted compartments; an upper one for unexposed plates and a lower one for exposed. After each shot, the two compartments moved in opposite directions to allow the exposed plate to drop down through a slit and to position the next plate ready for exposure.

Some manufacturers decided to give the photographer the choice of rollfilm or plates within the same camera. The Kodak Eureka mentioned above could take a cartridge rollfilm holder in place of the spare dark slides. Another Kodak camera, the No. 2 Bullet was initially designed for rollfilm but models from 1896 onwards could take a plateholder through a door in the side of the camera.

CAMERA : Facile
MANUFACTURER : Made for Followfield by Miall
DATE : 1889-*c*1900
COUNTRY OF ORIGIN : UK

CAMERA : Klito No. 3A
MANUFACTURER : G. Houghton & Sons
DATE : *c*1905-*c*1920
COUNTRY OF ORIGIN : UK

Graflex and Graphic Cameras

With many plate cameras the picture was focused and composed by looking at a ground-glass screen placed directly where the plate was to go. However, the single lens reflex (SLR) design uses a mirror at an angle of 45° to divert the image on to a screen on top of the camera. This allows the picture to be viewed right up to the moment of taking the shot, unlike a conventional plate camera, where loading the plate prevents the screen from being used. The design comes from seventeenth-century camera obscuras and was first used on a photographic camera by the English photographer Thomas Sutton in 1861. However, it did not come into general use until the 1890s when the speed of the dry plates made possible action photography, where the need to view the scene right up to the moment of taking the picture was extremely important.

One of the most influential SLR cameras to emerge during the 1890s was the Graflex made by Folmer & Schwing Mfg. Co. in New York. It was the first of a series of plate and rollfilm cameras of various designs which were to lead the way in certain professional fields of photography, particularly press work. The company was taken over by Eastman Kodak in 1905, but regained its independence in 1926. It underwent a series of name changes before finally settling on Graflex Inc. in 1945.

Along with their successful SLR Graflex cameras, the company produced some interesting non-SLR cameras. The No. 0 Graphic of 1909-1923 had a mirror on the viewfinder to make it

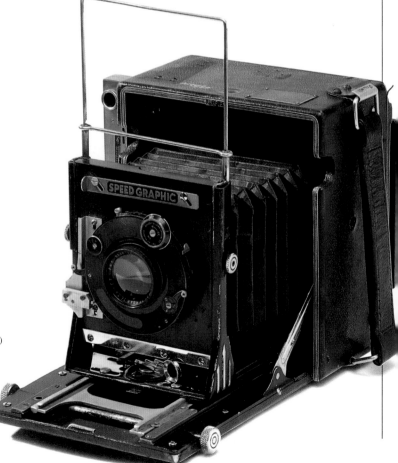

CAMERA : Anniversary Speed Graphic
MANUFACTURER : Folmer & Schwing Mfg. Co. (Graflex Inc.)
DATE : 1940-1946
COUNTRY OF ORIGIN : USA

CAMERA : No. 0 Graphic
MANUFACTURER : Folmer & Schwing Mfg. Co. (Graflex Inc.)
DATE : 1909-1923
COUNTRY OF ORIGIN : USA

look as if the photographer was taking a picture in a different direction to that in which the camera was actually pointing. This made it a popular choice for candid photography.

The non-SLR Speed Graphic cameras first came out in 1912 and were produced until 1973. For identification they are sub-divided into four types - Early (or Top Handle, on account of the carrying handle placed on the top of the camera), Pre-anniversary, Anniversary and Pacemaker. The Pre-anniversary model came out in 1928 and was immediately a success with press photographers. It was smaller and lighter than its predecessors, with a frame finder for following fast action. The

Anniversary model was produced from 1940-1946 and is considered by many to show the finest quality workmanship of any Speed Graphic camera. It was followed by the Pacemaker series which had three basic models known as the Speed, Crown and Century Graphics.

Graflex also produced two models of a monorail camera called the Graphic View (1941-1967). The monorail design first appeared during the last century, although it did not gain popularity until the 1950s. This design, which is used for large-format cameras, is almost universally preferred by today's professionals.

CAMERA : Pacemaker Speed Graphic
MANUFACTURER : Folmer & Schwing Mfg. Co. (Graflex Inc.)
DATE : 1947-1973
COUNTRY OF ORIGIN : USA

CAMERA : Anniversary Speed Graphic
MANUFACTURER : Folmer & Schwing Mfg. Co. (Graflex Inc.)
DATE : 1940-1946
COUNTRY OF ORIGIN : USA

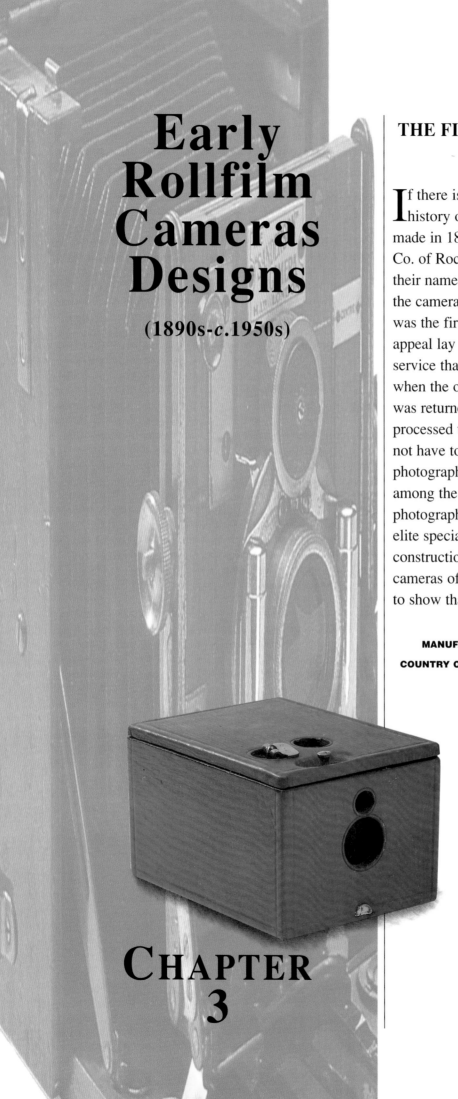

Early Rollfilm Cameras Designs

(1890s-*c*.1950s)

CHAPTER 3

THE FIRST KODAK AND BROWNIE CAMERAS

If there is one camera which stands out in the history of photography, it is The Kodak. It was made in 1888 by The Eastman Dry Plate & Film Co. of Rochester, New York, (who later changed their name to Eastman Kodak with the success of the camera). Although others had preceded it, it was the first successful rollfilm camera and its appeal lay in the full developing and printing service that went with it. It came ready loaded and, when the one hundred pictures had been taken, it was returned to Kodak who changed the film and processed the pictures. Thus the photographer did not have to know anything technical about photography, giving the camera a new market among the general public - from 1888 onwards, photography was no longer the domain of a few elite specialists. The camera was of a simple box construction similar to the cheaper hand plate cameras of the period, and it came tied and sealed to show that it was fresh from the factory.

CAMERA : Pocket Kodak
MANUFACTURER : Eastman Kodak
DATE : 1895-1900
COUNTRY OF ORIGIN : USA

CAMERA : Eastman Anniversary Kodak
MANUFACTURER : Eastman Kodak
DATE : May 1930
COUNTRY OF ORIGIN : USA

Initially the film used in The Kodak was on a paper base, but in 1889 Eastman introduced the first transparent celluloid-based film. In the same year, three more models of the camera appeared, taking larger pictures. The original model fetches a price beyond the budget of many collectors, but the three later models are not so highly priced. Also, there was a display replica of the original model made on its centenary in 1988 by Kodak Ltd., England, which can be purchased at very reasonable prices.

In 1895, Eastman introduced a tiny box rollfilm camera called, appropriately, the Pocket Kodak. Measuring just 10cm (4 inches) in length, this was the first Kodak camera to be mass produced. In the first year alone, more than 100,000 were sold - a figure which was quite extraordinary for its time.

Although these cameras were beginning to bring photography to the general public, they were still quite expensive for their day, so Eastman produced an even cheaper box camera in 1900. It was aimed at children and so was named after characters in the popular children's books of the period by Palmer Cox. The Brownie camera was an instant success and further models followed, some of which remained in production into the 1930s. The Brownie name continued to be used on Eastman Kodak cameras long after these early models; the last camera to bear the name was discontinued in 1982.

In May 1930, Eastman Kodak celebrated its 50th anniversary with a special box camera which was distributed free to twelve-year-old children. Based on the No. 2 Hawk-Eye, the Eastman Anniversary Kodak had a tan covering, gilt fittings and a gold foil badge on the side.

CAMERA : The Brownie
MANUFACTURER : Eastman Kodak
DATE : 1900-1901
COUNTRY OF ORIGIN : USA

CAMERA : The Kodak (Replica)
MANUFACTURER : Eastman Dry Plate & Film Co. (later
DATE : Eastman Kodak)
COUNTRY OF ORIGIN : 1888-1889 (Replica 1988)
USA (Replica UK)

BOX ROLLFILM CAMERAS

Seeing the success of the Eastman box rollfilm cameras, other manufacturers were keen to bring out cheap box cameras for the mass market.

A notable example was the Bull's-Eye designed by S. N. Turner and produced in 1892 by his company, the Boston Camera Mfg. Co. It incorporated a new idea about rollfilm which was to revolutionize photography. Until this time most cameras had needed to be loaded in a darkroom, but Turner rolled the film up with black backing paper so that it could be loaded in daylight. He put numbers on the back of the paper and a small red window in the back of the camera so that the photographer could see when he had wound on far enough. The idea was so good that Eastman bought out Turner's company, and the patent, in 1895, and the Bull's-Eye continued in production with some minor variations under the Eastman Kodak name.

The success of the simple box design can be seen from the long life-span of some of the cameras produced. For example, the Box Tengor first

CAMERA :	No. 2 Bull's-Eye
MANUFACTURER :	Eastman Kodak
DATE :	1895-1913
COUNTRY OF ORIGIN :	USA

appeared about 1925 and continued in production with Zeiss Ikon until 1956. Another 1950s example was the extraordinarily shaped Ensign Ful-Vue made in Britain between 1945-1950s.

As the popularity of photography increased, so did the size of the worldwide market for cameras. British and European manufacturers began to export cameras to Australia, where they were frequently renamed before they went on sale. For example, one of Australia's largest camera manufacturers, Harringtons Ltd. of Sydney, Melbourne and Brisbane, imported large numbers of cameras and gave them the trade name 'Ton'.

After the Second World War, another large Australian importing company was formed in Sydney, called Hanimex. Initially they imported cameras like the Hanimex Box camera of the mid-1950s from other manufacturers (Vredeborch of Germany in this case). But increasingly they turned to designing their own cameras and exporting them to the rest of the world.

CAMERA : Ensign Ful-Vue (postwar model)
MANUFACTURER : Ensign (Houghtons)
DATE : 1945-1950s
COUNTRY OF ORIGIN : UK

CAMERA : Box Tengor
MANUFACTURER : Zeiss Ikon
DATE : c1925-1956
COUNTRY OF ORIGIN : Germany

31

FOLDING POCKET KODAKS

CAMERA : No. O Folding Pocket Kodak
MANUFACTURER : Eastman Kodak
DATE : 1902-1906
COUNTRY OF ORIGIN : USA

Although very popular and cheap to make, the box design did have the disadvantage that it would not fold to a more compact size so, in 1897, Eastman Kodak introduced a range of folding rollfilm cameras called the Folding Pocket Kodaks (FPKs). They were produced in vast numbers throughout the early part of the twentieth century and are among the most commonly seen cameras on the collectors' markets worldwide.

The early models had struts on which the lens panel pulled out from the camera body; and the entire camera, including the lens panel, was covered with leather. The original model had brass struts and four windows on the lens panel (only two of which were actually used for viewfinders). The brass was replaced in 1898 by Nickel-plating, which was being used increasingly around the turn of the century. This original model was called simply the Folding Pocket Kodak, but was renamed the No. 1 Folding Pocket Kodak, model

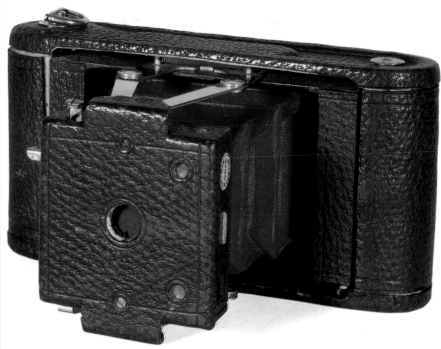

CAMERA : Folding Pocket Kodak
MANUFACTURER : Eastman Kodak
DATE : 1897-1899
COUNTRY OF ORIGIN : USA

CAMERA : No. 3A Folding Pocket Kodak
MANUFACTURER : Eastman Kodak
DATE : 1903-1915
COUNTRY OF ORIGIN : USA

B, in 1899 when other models appeared. The number given to a model indicates its film size, so a No. 4 FPK takes larger pictures than a No. 3. In 1902 Kodak decided to bring out a smaller size than the original and so had little choice but to call it the No. 0. Some collectors have mistakenly thought that this must represent the first model since it has the lowest number, but the numbering system has nothing to do with the order in which

the cameras were introduced.

The design gradually developed, along with the materials used in construction, and both can be used as a rough guide to dating. In 1899, the No. 2 introduced a flap of metal which folded up over the lens as the camera shut, thus protecting it from damage. This typical folding camera design was to replace the original strut design on all models over the next few years. Around 1905 the leather

CAMERA : No. 3A Autographic Kodak
MANUFACTURER : Special with Coupled Rangefinder
Eastman Kodak
DATE : 1916-1937
COUNTRY OF ORIGIN : USA

covering on the lens panel of the earlier models was dropped in favour of a plain wooden or metal finish; and over the next ten years, all remaining wooden lens panels were replaced with metal ones. Finally, a feature called the Autographic feature appeared on all models from 1914 onwards and they were renamed the Autographic Kodaks (as we shall see in the following pages).

Many variations of each model existed, with the range of prices according to the quality of its particular lens, shutter etc. Regional variations occurred also, so, for example, those on the British market are more likely to be found with lenses of British or European manufacture. One model of particular note is the No. 3A Autographic Kodak Special (1916-1937 model), the first camera ever with a coupled rangefinder for focusing.

AUTOGRAPHIC KODAKS

We have all looked at some of our old films and found that one or two pictures look familiar but we cannot quite place where we took them! Unfortunately, few of us think to note down what we have photographed while it is fresh on our minds. The American Henry J. Gaisman invented a system, called the Autographic feature, to overcome this problem by writing the information on the film itself immediately after each exposure. He proposed that a special opaque tissue should be rolled up between the film and the backing paper. This tissue could be rendered translucent by pressure from a metal stylus, so that light filtering through the backing paper would expose the film and show the writing. The system needed a special window in the back of

CAMERA : Vanity Kodak
MANUFACTURER : Eastman Kodak
DATE : 1928-1933
COUNTRY OF ORIGIN : USA

the camera protected by a light-tight flap which could be opened to access the film.

Eastman Kodak paid Gaisman for the rights to the patents and used the feature from 1914 to the early 1930s. Care should be taken when dating Kodak rollfilm cameras, as conversion backs were available for the earlier FPK models, so pre-1914 models exist with the Autographic feature.

Three styles of the feature were used: from 1914-1916 the metal stylus lay in a recess in the flap covering the window and both were held in place by a metal strip; from 1916-1920s the stylus lay along the edge of the flap, held in place by a spring; and during the 1920s some models had a sliding door instead of a flap and the stylus was held at the side of the lens panel.

Kodak continued to build on the successes of their early folding rollfilm cameras with the new Autographic models. The Vest Pocket Autographic Kodak, which used the film size 127 introduced in 1912, was one of the biggest selling cameras of its day. This film size continued to be popular for many years.

From the late 1920s into the 1930s, cameras went through a period of being rather more decorative than before. Kodak produced three

CAMERA : Vest Pocket Autographic Kodak
MANUFACTURER : Eastman Kodak
DATE : 1915-1926
COUNTRY OF ORIGIN : USA

CAMERA : Boy Scout Kodak
MANUFACTURER : Eastman Kodak
DATE : 1929-1934
COUNTRY OF ORIGIN : USA & UK

interesting examples, all for 127 film size and based on Vest Pocket models. The Vanity Kodak (1928-1933), advertised as 'The Modern Camera for the Modern Girl', came in a variety of colours with the metal parts enamelled in the same colour and a matching silk-lined case. The Boy Scout and Girl Scout Kodaks (Girl Guide Kodak in the UK) had the insignia of those organizations enamelled on the baseplates.

CAMERA : Girl Guide Kodak
MANUFACTURER : Kodak Ltd.
DATE : 1931-1935
COUNTRY OF ORIGIN : UK

FOLDING ROLLFILM CAMERAS

With the success of the Eastman Kodak folding rollfilm cameras, it was hardly surprising that other manufacturers started to produce very similar cameras. With the exception of the Autographic feature for which only Kodak held the patents, they frequently looked very similar in style and design.

In America one of Kodak's main competitors was the company Ansco of Binghampton, New York, which merged with the American side of the German company Agfa to form Agfa-Ansco in 1928. Among their many folding rollfilm cameras

CAMERA	:	No. 3A Folding Ansco
MANUFACTURER	:	Ansco
DATE	:	c1914-1932
COUNTRY OF ORIGIN	:	USA

was the unusual Ansco Automatic 1A of c1925 which could take all of its six shots in just six seconds, using a clockwork motor drive wound by a key built into the camera back.

During the interwar period, Britain's largest camera manufacturer, Houghton-Butcher, was formed by the merger of the two well-known names. The Carbine series of folding rollfilm cameras came from the Butcher side of the merger and between 1927 and 1936 several unusual tropical models were made. They had tan bellows and a bronzed brass body, and came with the good quality Tessar lens and Compur shutter.

Zeiss Ikon produced many folding rollfilm cameras in Germany for distribution there and abroad. They offered a bewildering number of models and variations, but these can usually be sorted out by looking for the unique factory code

CAMERA :	Ensign Carbine Tropical Model
MANUFACTURER :	Houghton-Butcher Ltd.
DATE :	1927-1936
COUNTRY OF ORIGIN :	UK

which was often embossed in the leather covering. They take the form of 510/2, where the first number indicates the type of camera (in this case the Bob of 1937-1938) and the second part of the number gives the size of the picture taken by that particular model, so '2' represents the popular size of 6 x 9cm (2.4 x 3.5 inches). These numbers help to distinguish the types when there is any confusion over the names used, as the cameras did not always sell under the same name in different countries. For example, the Bob sold in Great Britain under the name Nettar, but the factory code 510 occurs on both name variants, thus making identification possible.

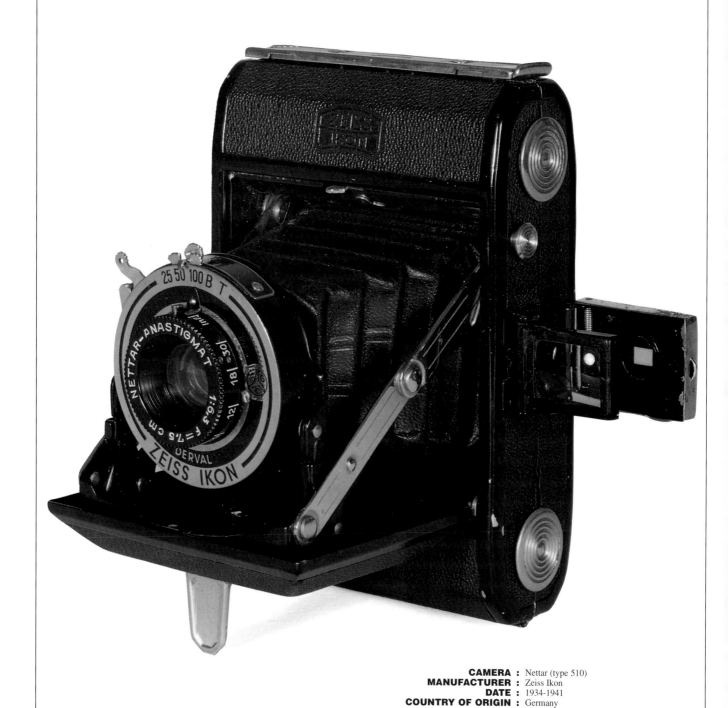

CAMERA : Nettar (type 510)
MANUFACTURER : Zeiss Ikon
DATE : 1934-1941
COUNTRY OF ORIGIN : Germany

Later Rollfilm and non-35mm

(c1890s onwards)

CHAPTER 4

SLR ROLLFILM CAMERAS

As mentioned in Chapter 3 with the Graflex cameras, the single lens reflex (SLR) design began to appear on a commercial scale around the turn of the century. Various cameras were manufactured along broadly the same designs as seen in the Graflex models for both plate and rollfilm. A typical example is the Ensign Roll Film Reflex made by Houghton-Butcher in England during the 1920s.

In 1921, a camera manufacturer called Ihagee in Dresden (a German Mecca for camera manufacture at the time) brought out a humble SLR box rollfilm camera called the Roll-Paff. It took pictures 6cm (2¼ inches) square on 120 film,

CAMERA : Ensign Roll Film Reflex
MANUFACTURER : Houghton-Butcher Ltd.
DATE : 1920s
COUNTRY OF ORIGIN : UK

a size which is still in use today. As we shall see, Ihagee's later SLR cameras were to have a major influence on the history of camera design.

The Reflex-Korelle, manufactured by another Dresden firm, Franz Kochmann, was introduced in 1935 and is sometimes incorrectly claimed by collectors to be the first 6cm (2¼ inches) square SLR 120 rollfilm camera. It should not be confused with the Meister Korelle (called Master Reflex on the American market) made some years later by WEFO of Dresden. This camera looks very similar superficially, but is of a different construction.

The year 1948 saw the introduction of a camera which was the forerunner of some of the best-known rollfilm SLRs of today - the Hasselblad 1600F. Unlike later Hasselblads, this model had a focal-plane shutter and was capable of a top speed

CAMERA : Roll-Paff
MANUFACTURER : Ihagee
DATE : 1921
COUNTRY OF ORIGIN : Germany

of 1/1600 second. This proved to be a little too fast and operational problems meant that it had to be reduced for the second model, the 1000F of 1952-1957.

The Hasselblad family firm in Sweden dated back to 1841 and sold photographic supplies from 1887 onwards. However, the SLR cameras of today are produced by the company set up in 1941 by Victor Hasselblad to manufacture aerial cameras. The company used a method of encoding the year of manufacture in the serial number, something which is not uncommon and can be a great help to collectors. In Hasselblad cameras the serial number is preceded by two letters chosen from 'VH PICTURES' which encode the year by representing the digits '12 34567890'.

CAMERA : Hasselblad 1600F
MANUFACTURER : Hasselblad
DATE : 1948-1952
COUNTRY OF ORIGIN : Sweden

CAMERA : Reflex-Korelle
MANUFACTURER : Franz Kochmann
DATE : 1935
COUNTRY OF ORIGIN : Germany

NEW DEVELOPMENTS

The German company Ihagee began production in 1932 of a revolutionary design of SLR for 127 ('Vest Pocket') rollfilm. Called the Exakta, it was the first camera to bear a strong resemblance to the 35mm SLRs of today. It was much smaller and more compact than previous SLR designs and became an immediate success. In 1933, they introduced the Exakta B with a focal-plane shutter capable of 12 seconds to 1/1000 second, a range unrivalled until the early 1970s. The Exakta Vest Pocket and 35mm cameras are frequently the subject of specialist collections.

During the 1930s, manufacturers were beginning to bring in new techniques of mass production using a wider range of materials than had previously been seen. The Purma Special made by R. F. Hunter Ltd, England in 1937 was constructed of Bakelite and metal and had a non-

CAMERA : Purma Special
MANUFACTURER : R. F. Hunter Ltd.
DATE : 1937
COUNTRY OF ORIGIN : UK

CAMERA : Exakta A
MANUFACTURER : Ihagee
DATE : 1932-c1940
COUNTRY OF ORIGIN : Germany

SLR viewfinder with a plastic lens. It also had an unusual shutter with just three speeds which were controlled by gravity. A different speed was obtained depending on whether the camera was held horizontally, or vertically in one direction or the other. It took 127 film and, needless to say, square pictures, so that turning the camera for different speeds had no effect on the image.

Although not for rollfilm, three other non-35mm cameras are worthy of mention here. They are all of SLR design and it is this which is so unusual about them, because they are for film sizes which are usually associated with simpler designs. The 126 easy-to-load film cartridge was introduced in 1963 and, based on its considerable success, the smaller 110 cartridge appeared in 1972. The instamatic cameras using these film sizes are generally not considered collectible classics but the odd exception, based on an unusual or innovative design, does exist.

CAMERA : Contaflex 126 (type 10.1102)
MANUFACTURER : Zeiss Ikon
DATE : 1968
COUNTRY OF ORIGIN : Germany

CAMERA : Kodak Instamatic Reflex (type 062)
MANUFACTURER : Kodak AG
DATE : 1968-1970
COUNTRY OF ORIGIN : Germany

In 1968, two SLR 126 cameras appeared with interchangeable lenses, a feature which is more commonly associated with cameras for the serious amateur and professional rather than for instamatics. They were the Kodak Instamatic Reflex and the Contaflex 126. The Kodak camera was available with a range of good-quality lenses which had been first used for their 35mm Retina Reflex cameras. The Contaflex 126 had a range of four lenses, and a complete outfit of camera plus all the lenses fetches much higher price than the camera plus the most common 45mm lens alone.

The Minolta 110 Zoom SLR was the first SLR for 110 film and was produced in 1976. It had automatic aperture-priority exposure and a non-interchangeable zoom lens.

CAMERA : Minolta 110 Zoom SLR
MANUFACTURER : Minolta
DATE : 1976
COUNTRY OF ORIGIN : Japan

ROLLEIFLEXES AND ROLLEICORDS

There is an alternative to the SLR design and that is the twin lens reflex, 'TLR'. Instead of the mirror lying behind the taking lens as in the SLRs, there is a second viewing lens and mirror situated above the taking lens. The design appeared in the last century but tended to be too cumbersome for the plate cameras of the day. However, with the smaller rollfilms of this century, TLRs began to reappear around the 1930s. One company has become synonymous with rollfilm TLRs - Franke & Heidecke (later known as Rollei).

The firm was founded in Brunswick, Germany, by Paul Franke and Reinhold Heidecke in 1920, initially to produce high-quality cameras for

CAMERA : Rolleiflex (original model)
MANUFACTURER : Franke & Heidecke
DATE : 1929-1932
COUNTRY OF ORIGIN : Germany

CAMERA : Rolleicord I
MANUFACTURER : Franke & Heidecke
DATE : 1933-1936
COUNTRY OF ORIGIN : Germany

stereoscopic photography. In 1928, they made the first prototypes of the Rolleiflex TLR camera, which went on sale in the following year. It originally took 6cm (2¼ inches) square pictures on 117 size film, although some cameras were modified to take 120 film as well. This camera was the beginning of a line of over thirty major models, all of which are highly collectible.

In 1933, Franke & Heidecke started a cheaper range of cameras as an alternative to the Rolleiflexes, called Rolleicords. Although not as highly regarded by collectors, the first model in the range, which is decorated with a nickel-plated art-deco design, often finds its way into collections.

Both Rolleiflexes and Rolleicords can pose identification problems because, until the 1960s, only the camera name appeared; there was no identification of the model. A combination of the serial number and features of the camera is the only secure means of identification. However, one useful indicator with Rolleiflexes is the style of

CAMERA : Rolleiflex Old Standard
MANUFACTURER : Franke & Heidecke
DATE : 1932-1938
COUNTRY OF ORIGIN : Germany

CAMERA : Rolleiflex Automat (Automatic Rolleiflex)
MANUFACTURER : Franke & Heidecke
DATE : 1937-1949
COUNTRY OF ORIGIN : Germany

nameplate. With the early models, the name was etched on the plate and filled with white paint; in later models (late 1930s onwards) the nameplate was cast with raised letters.

The more important models of Rolleiflexes include the Old Standard model of 1932 which replaced the 117 size film with 120. The word 'Old' was not used at the time but has been added by collectors to distinguish it from the New Standard model of 1939. The 120 size was used on most models, with the exception of a few smaller models called Baby Rolleiflexes. Some later cameras, including the 1969-1980 model of the popular 3.5F, could take the longer 220 film size for more pictures per film.

The Rolleiflex Automat of 1937 (known as the Automatic Rolleiflex in America) was a landmark model as it introduced fully coupled winding and shutter cocking. This made the camera quicker and easier to use and assured its popularity among professional photographers.

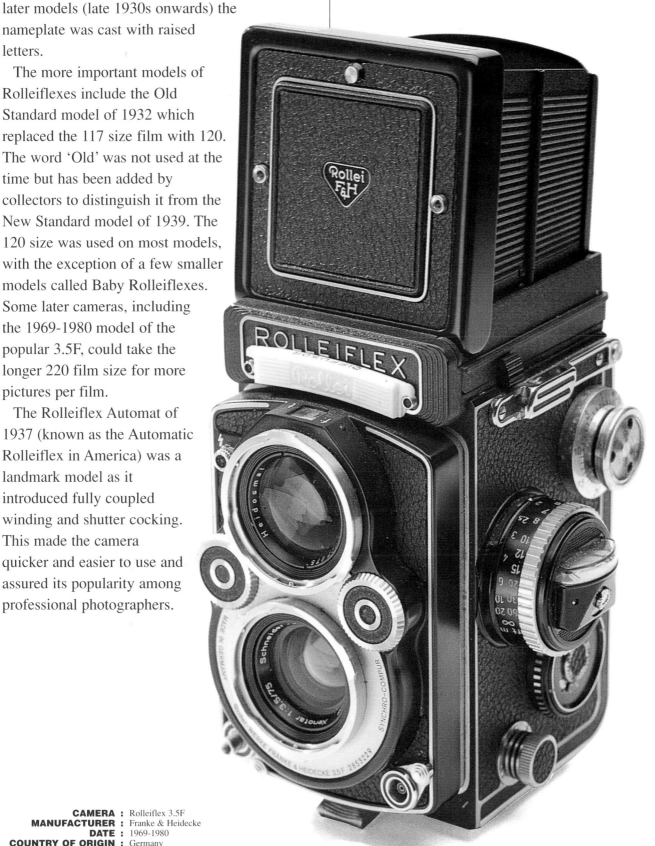

CAMERA : Rolleiflex 3.5F
MANUFACTURER : Franke & Heidecke
DATE : 1969-1980
COUNTRY OF ORIGIN : Germany

TLR ROLLFILM CAMERAS

With the success of Rolleiflexes, other manufacturers turned their attention to the TLR design for rollfilm cameras.

Among them was a Japanese company formed in 1928, the same year as the prototype Rolleiflex. Later to be known as Minolta, they produced Japan's first TLR camera in 1936. Although called the Minoltaflex, it has only the word Minolta on the front. This is useful for distinguishing this model from the later Minoltaflexes. The main body was based on the Rolleicord and it had a unique shutter release and lock to prevent double exposures. Minolta produced many TLR rollfilm cameras over the next thirty years, among them the Minolta Autochord of 1955.

An interesting German TLR was made by Welta Kamera-Werke in 1934 and called the Perfekta. It had an unusual folding design based on lazy-tong struts of a criss-cross design which made it a very compact size when it was not in use.

After the Second World War, the Russian camera manufacturer GOMZ started to manufacture what must be the longest surviving

CAMERA : Brillant
MANUFACTURER : Voigtländer & Sohn
DATE : 1933
COUNTRY OF ORIGIN : Germany

CAMERA : Perfekta
MANUFACTURER : Welta
DATE : 1934
COUNTRY OF ORIGIN : Germany

TLR camera. The Lubitel is still available today as a cheap introduction to medium-format rollfilm photography. It was a copy of the Brillant, which was manufactured in Germany by Voigtländer & Sohn and is frequently found on the collectors' market.

Another TLR camera which survives today is made by the Japanese manufacturer Mamiya. Their line of TLR cameras started just before the 1950s with the Mamiyaflex Junior. Among their early models was the Mamiyaflex Automatic-A, which was the first Japanese camera of this type to have an automatic stop for winding on film.

This made winding-on quicker, as it was unnecessary to watch the red window for the next number on the film to appear. In 1957 they introduced the first of their 'C' range of Mamiyaflexes aimed at the professional market, and it is this range which continues today. The Mamiyaflex C introduced interchangeable lenses, a feature which gives the camera some of the versatility of the SLR design. However, many TLR cameras do not have this feature; it is expensive, since both the viewing and the taking lens need to be replaced, plus the shutter in the case of the Mamiyaflex C range.

CAMERA : Minolta Autochord
MANUFACTURER : Chiyoda Kogaku (Minolta)
DATE : 1955-1965
COUNTRY OF ORIGIN : Japan

CAMERA : Lubitel 2
MANUFACTURER : GOMZ (Lomo)
DATE : 1963 - present
COUNTRY OF ORIGIN : Russia

35 mm Cameras

3 5mm film was first introduced for movie pictures and had become a standard size by the First World War. Several camera manufacturers thought about using this readily available film stock for still cameras; but the early attempts were not very successful because the early 35mm films were not of a high enough quality.

CHAPTER 5

Among the early 35mm cameras was the Debrie Sept, which was made in Paris in 1921. It took film loaded into its own special cassettes and was designed to be used as either a still or a movie camera. For the latter, it had a built-in clockwork motor, but it is debatable how good it was for movie work as it could only take 250 frames (about 10-15 seconds) before running out of film!

Just before the First World War, a German design engineer and keen mountaineer, Oskar Barnack, had been working on a small camera for use in the mountains. He made a prototype in 1913 but it was not until 1924 that the camera went into production at the factory where he worked: E. Leitz Optische Werke, Wetzlar, Germany. It was called the Leica from the initials of 'LEItz CAmera' and took pictures of the size 24 x 36mm (1 x 1½ inches) which was to become the standard for 35mm still photography. Further Leica models appeared, most notably the Leica I Model C (1931, the first with interchangeable lenses), the Leica II (1932, the first with a coupled rangefinder), and the Leica III (1933, the first with slow shutter speeds).

With the popularity of the Leica camera, other manufacturers began to move into 35mm in earnest during the 1930s. The main competitor to the Leica was Zeiss Ikon's Contax camera. The first model was produced in 1932 and had a built-in coupled rangefinder which spanned the entire top of the camera, unlike the Leica II, whose rangefinder had a much shorter base.

Various copies of the Leica and Contax cameras were produced, notably in Japan and the former Soviet Union. The early Japanese rangefinders from Canon and Nikon are currently fetching very high prices on the collectors' market. However, the Ukrainian copies such as the Kiev and Fed, and the Russian Zorki are still very affordable. One interesting model of the Kiev was produced in the early 1960s for the U.S. market without any identifying name on it, because of American reluctance to buy Soviet goods during the Cold War. Because it looks just like a Zeiss Ikon Contax IIa or IIIa, it is sometimes incorrectly called the 'No-Name Contax'.

CAMERA : Debrie Sept
MANUFACTURER : A. Debrie
DATE : 1921-1927
COUNTRY OF ORIGIN : France

53

CAMERA : Contax I
MANUFACTURER : Zeiss Ikon
DATE : 1932-1936
COUNTRY OF ORIGIN : Germany

CAMERA : Leica II
MANUFACTURER : Ernst Leitz
DATE : 1932-1948
COUNTRY OF ORIGIN : Germany

CAMERA : Kiev 3A
MANUFACTURER : Kiev Arsenal
DATE : 1956-1958
COUNTRY OF ORIGIN : Ukraine

35mm SLR CAMERAS

The early 35mm cameras used a rangefinder for focusing, but it was not long before manufacturers began to look at the possibility of using the single lens reflex design. As has already been seen (on pages 22 and 34), the SLR design had been used before in non-35mm cameras, including the popular Exakta Vest Pocket models. So it was not surprising when Ihagee produced a 35mm version of the Exakta in 1936. It was probably not quite the first 35mm SLR as the Russian camera called 'Sport' (Cnopm in cyrillic letters) was reputedly produced a year earlier. However, the Kine Exakta was certainly the first to be widely used.

The early 35mm SLRs did not have the now-familiar pentaprism on top of the camera to turn the picture the correct way round in the viewfinder. It was not until 1949 that two cameras appeared on the market with this feature - the German Contax S and the Italian Rectaflex. The Contax S is considered to be the first, as it was patented at an earlier date. It was manufactured by the former Zeiss Ikon factory in Dresden, which was by then in the newly formed East Germany.

CAMERA : Contax D
MANUFACTURER : VEB Pentacon
DATE : 1953
COUNTRY OF ORIGIN : Germany

CAMERA : Kine Exakta (with added PC socket on front)
MANUFACTURER : Ihagee
DATE : 1936-1948
COUNTRY OF ORIGIN : Germany

The West German Zeiss Ikon factory at Stuttgart took legal proceedings against the East German factory and, after many years, won the sole rights to use the names Zeiss and Contax. These legal arguments typified the post-war era in the German photographic industry and have led to some interesting name changes on cameras during the 1950s. For example, a later model of the Contax S, called initially the Contax D, became the Pentacon D after the legal battle.

Other German manufacturers involved with legal battles at the time included Ihagee, but production of the highly successful Exakta range of cameras continued in their Dresden factory throughout the 1950s and 60s. Among these was the Exakta V (Varex) of 1950, which was the first 35mm SLR with an interchangeable pentaprism.

The Japanese continued to make 35mm rangefinder cameras and, in 1952, their first SLR came on to the market. It was the Asahiflex, which was the forerunner of the well-known Pentax range. In 1959 another Japanese company, Nippon Kogaku, turned to the SLR design with their Nikon F. It was truly a classic camera which had a great influence on professionals and amateurs alike. Before the Nikon F, European camera manufacturers dominated the 35mm market; after this landmark camera the Japanese were to dominate.

CAMERA : Asahiflex IIB
MANUFACTURER : Asahi Kogaku
DATE : 1954
COUNTRY OF ORIGIN : Japan

CAMERA : Nikon F
MANUFACTURER : Nippon Kogaku (Nikon)
DATE : 1959
COUNTRY OF ORIGIN : Japan

UNUSUAL 35mm CAMERAS

Although the two major designs of 35mm camera were the rangefinder and SLR, there were many cameras produced which had slightly more unusual designs. Whenever a camera has a slightly off-beat or innovative design, it is quite likely that it will be collectible - a point to note if you are interested in collecting new cameras of today as an investment for tomorrow.

The Robot 1 camera produced by Otto Berning & Co. of Düsseldorf, Germany, was unusual in that it contained an automatic film advance. This feature has become commonplace on today's cameras, but in 1934 when the Robot appeared it was most unusual. It also had a built-in filter which could be moved into its place behind the lens by a switch on the front of the camera. Since most filters are placed on the front of the lens this was, again, a novel feature. The Robot range of cameras is still in production today for professional use in surveillance and instrument recording - as some speeding motorists have found to their cost!

The Argus C range of cameras produced in Michigan, USA, can hardly be said to be the most beautiful of designs - and yet this very fact makes them collectible. Affectionately known as 'The

CAMERA : Retina Type 117
MANUFACTURER : Kodak AG
DATE : 1934-1935
COUNTRY OF ORIGIN : Germany

Brick' on account of its shape, the first model came out in 1938, and the Argus C3 model continued in production until 1966. They were advertised in the UK under the name Minca instead of Argus.

The folding design which was so popular for rollfilm cameras throughout this century was only used on one well-known range of 35mm cameras. This was Kodak's early Retina and Retinette

cameras, produced from 1934 to 1958, when the company dropped this design. The Retina 1 Type 117 (1934) was Kodak's first 35mm camera and it introduced a new type of film cassette, which Kodak designated 135. This is now the standard 35mm cassette in use today. The budget-priced Retinette range of cameras was introduced in 1939 with the Type 147. Both the Retinas and Retinettes were manufactured solely in Germany

CAMERA : Robot 1
MANUFACTURER : Otto Berning & Co.
DATE : 1934-1939
COUNTRY OF ORIGIN : Germany

CAMERA : Periflex
MANUFACTURER : K. G. Corfield
DATE : 1953-1957
COUNTRY OF ORIGIN : UK

by Kodak AG.

A most unusual design of reflex viewfinder appeared on the British-made Periflex camera in 1953. A tiny mirror was pushed down into the camera to reflect just a small part of the picture up on to a focusing screen, and then raised just before the exposure was made. This periscope-like arrangement had to be operated manually on early models, but was automatic with later ones.

One tends to think of the twin lens reflex design as being mainly used on rollfilm cameras during this century (see pages 38-41). However, a few 35mm cameras have been of this design. The Zeiss Ikon Contaflex TLR of 1935 was the first such camera, and the only one to have interchangeable lenses. It was an impressive camera which was also the first to have a built-in photo-electric meter and the first to use a van

CAMERA : Argus C3 ('The Brick')
MANUFACTURER : Argus Inc.
DATE : 1939-1966
COUNTRY OF ORIGIN : USA

Albada reflecting frame finder (a type of viewfinder useful in action photography). However, it was bulky at 1.4kg (3⅛lb) and, because it was hand-built and extensively tested in the factory, it was very expensive - nearly three times the price of a Leica.

The TLR design was not the only unusual 35mm design to be experimented with. The Werra, made by Carl Zeiss Jena from c1955 onwards, had several intriguing features. The lens cap reversed to fit over the lens when the camera was not in use, and there were no knobs or wind-on levers on top of the camera, since advancing the film was done by turning a ring on the lens barrel. The models from the first five years of production had an olive green covering, but later

CAMERA : Contaflex TLR
MANUFACTURER : Zeiss Ikon
DATE : 1935
COUNTRY OF ORIGIN : Germany

CAMERA : Olympus OM-1
MANUFACTURER : Olympus Kogaku
DATE : 1972
COUNTRY OF ORIGIN : Japan

CAMERA : Werra
MANUFACTURER : Carl Zeiss Jena
DATE : c1955
COUNTRY OF ORIGIN : Germany

models were black. Also additions were made to the basic design, such as a coupled rangefinder, interchangeable lenses and a built-in meter.

The early 35mm SLRs had a certain bulk, but in 1972 Olympus announced a camera which had all the features expected of an SLR, but within a lightweight, small frame. The Olympus M-1 quickly had its name changed to OM-1 because there had already been a Leica M-1; and since very few were produced with the original name,

they fetch about twice the price on the collectors' market.

Disposable cameras come ready-loaded with film and are destroyed when it is taken out for processing. Some collectors have started to collect them since, naturally, they become rare as soon as production ceases. Some are packaged specially for a promotion, while others, such as the Kodak Fun Panoramic, take special pictures (see page 60 for more information about panoramic cameras).

CAMERA : Fun Panoramic disposable camera
MANUFACTURER : Eastman Kodak
DATE : Present
COUNTRY OF ORIGIN : USA

CAMERA : Memo (1927 type)
MANUFACTURER : Ansco
DATE : 1927
COUNTRY OF ORIGIN : USA

HALF-FRAME CAMERAS

The standard size of a 35mm still negative is 36 x 24mm (1 1/2 x 1 inches) but several manufacturers have experimented with other sizes. In particular the size 18 x 24mm (3/4 x 1 inch), which was used in the original 35mm movie cameras, has been used on several occasions. Since it is half the standard size, it is known as half-frame.

Several of the early 35mm cameras were of this type, for example the Debrie Sept already mentioned at the start of this chapter. Another early example is the Memo made in the United States by Ansco. It was a wooden camera of an unusual vertical style which first came out in 1927. Ansco produced several cameras over a long period with the name Memo and collectors should specify which model is being referred to. Otherwise there is likely to be some confusion! This one is known as the Memo (1927 type).

Another American half-frame camera was the odd-looking Univex Mercury made in New York from 1938 onwards. The bulge on the top of the camera was needed to accommodate a rotating

CAMERA : Univex Mercury Model CC
MANUFACTURER : Universal Camera Corp.
DATE : 1938-1942
COUNTRY OF ORIGIN : USA

blade type of focal-plane shutter which was too big to fit inside the camera. This also explains why it was only a half-frame camera, as the shutter blade would have had to be even larger for a full-size negative.

Half-frame really came into its own during the 1960s. By this time film technology had developed greatly, giving higher quality prints even off the smaller negative. One range of cameras led the way during this period - the Olympus Pen cameras. The original model came out in 1959 and was a simple compact camera which could be slipped easily into a pocket. Eighteen more models based on this design came out over the next twenty years with increasing automation. None were SLRs, but in 1963 Olympus brought out the Pen F, the first 35mm half-frame SLR. Four models of the F series were made and they had a complete SLR system of interchangeable lenses, equipment for close-up work, etc.

Other manufacturers followed Olympus' lead, notably Canon, who produced a series of half-frame cameras during the 1960s. Two types were made - the Demi, of which there were several models, and the Dial 35 with just two models. Both appeared for the first time in 1963 but the Dial, with a spring-driven motor drive, had the most interesting design: the spring housing extended under the camera to form a handle.

CAMERA : Olympus Pen (original model)
MANUFACTURER : Olympus Kogaku
DATE : 1959
COUNTRY OF ORIGIN : Japan

CAMERA : Olympus Pen F
MANUFACTURER : Olympus Kogaku
DATE : 1963
COUNTRY OF ORIGIN : Japan

CAMERA : Dial 35
MANUFACTURER : Canon
DATE : 1963-1967
COUNTRY OF ORIGIN : Japan

INCREASING AUTOMATION

Automatic exposure had first appeared on the Super Kodak Six-20, a rollfilm camera of 1938. Over the next thirty years many cameras of varying degrees of automation were manufactured. One of the simplest ways of automating exposure is to fix the shutter speed according to the type of film and then to vary only the aperture. Several 35mm cameras working on this kind of principle appeared c1960, among them the Agfa Optima. It fixed the shutter speed at between 1/30 and 1/500 for films of speeds 10 to 200 ASA, leaving the meter to control only the aperture.

The early camera meters were placed on the outside of the camera, but this has the disadvantage that it fails to read the actual amount of light coming through the lens, which may differ if there is a filter in place or with certain attachments used for close-up work. Through the lens (TTL) metering gets over this by placing the meter behind the lens and measuring the light coming into the camera. The first coupled TTL metering appeared on a sub-miniature camera, the German Mec-16 SB made by Feinoptisches Werk, but the first 35mm SLR to have it was the Topcon RE Super which was introduced in 1963. This Japanese camera was made by Tokyo Kogaku and

CAMERA : Agfa Optima
MANUFACTURER : Agfa
DATE : 1959-1963
COUNTRY OF ORIGIN : Germany

CAMERA : Topcon RE Super
MANUFACTURER : Tokyo Kogaku
DATE : 1963
COUNTRY OF ORIGIN : Japan

CAMERA : Vitrona
MANUFACTURER : Voigtländer & Sohn
DATE : 1964
COUNTRY OF ORIGIN : Germany

was also sold under the name variant Topcon Super D.

Designing a fully automatic focal-plane shutter is not easy, but in 1967 Konishiroku Kogaku succeeded with their Konica Autoreflex camera. It was capable of taking pictures of either full or half-frame sizes and several models were made throughout the 1970s.

The 1960s saw the introduction of another feature which has become commonplace on today's cameras: built-in electronic flash. It first appeared on the Voigtländer Vitrona in 1964 but the need for a handle containing the supply of batteries made the camera somewhat unwieldy to use.

The latest significant advance in 35mm camera design came in 1978 when the Konica C35AF, the first camera with autofocus, was introduced. During the 1980s others followed, notably the Canon T80, which was the first SLR able to use autofocus lenses, and the Minolta 7000. The latter was the first truly Autofocus SLR with the mechanism lying within the body of the camera, not in the lens as with the Canon.

CAMERA : Minolta 7000
MANUFACTURER : Minolta
DATE : 1985
COUNTRY OF ORIGIN : Japan

Specialist Cameras

Many collectors decide to specialize in one particular theme for their collections rather than to attempt to collect from all the different types of camera ever made. This chapter gives four of the most common themes which can form the basis of a collection _ instant, miniature, stereo and panoramic cameras.

INSTANT CAMERAS

The idea of an instant camera is that the processing of the picture is done inside the camera, cutting out the need for a darkroom. Suggestions for such a camera started at the very beginning of photography itself, but it was not

CHAPTER 6

CAMERA :	Polaroid Land 95
MANUFACTURER :	Polaroid
DATE :	1948-1953
COUNTRY OF ORIGIN :	USA

until 1853 that the first commercial camera was manufactured incorporating the idea, based on a design by the Englishman Frederick Scott Archer.

Several cameras followed throughout the nineteenth century, but they were always rather specialized and it was not until this century that an effort was made to bring instant photography to the general public. The first attempt at a cheap, mass-produced instant camera came in 1936 from a New York company called

Photo-See. This was a simple cardboard box camera which produced a print in just five minutes. The camera sold for under $2 but it was not commercially successful. However, the next instant camera to come from America took photography by storm.

Designed by the American scientist and inventor, Dr. Edwin H. Land, and manufactured by Polaroid of Cambridge, Massachusetts, the Polaroid Land Camera Model 95 went on sale in 1948. It was the first instant camera which did not require the use of bottles of chemicals, since the

necessary chemicals were incorporated into a tiny pod at one end of the print. After exposure, the negative and print were pulled through rollers together, which burst the pod and spread out the chemicals evenly. Just one minute later a flap in the camera back could be opened and the finished print peeled off the negative, which was discarded.

Further improvements were made both to the Polaroid cameras and to the process. In 1963, Polaroid were the first to produce a fully automatic electronic shutter with their Automatic 100 model, and they marketed their first colour film in the same year. The model SX-70 of 1972 was of a revolutionary SLR design and is viewed as a landmark in Polaroid's history.

Polaroid cameras are very reasonably priced on the collectors' market, particularly in America where supply outstrips demand. European prices tend to be higher but they are still some of the cheapest collectible cameras around and make an interesting thematic collection.

CAMERA : Photo-See
MANUFACTURER : Photo-See Corp.
DATE : 1936
COUNTRY OF ORIGIN : USA

CAMERA : Polaroid Land Automatic 100
MANUFACTURER : Polaroid
DATE : 1963-1966
COUNTRY OF ORIGIN : USA

CAMERA : Polaroid Land SX-70
MANUFACTURER : Polaroid
DATE : 1972-1977
COUNTRY OF ORIGIN : USA

MINIATURE AND SUB-MINIATURE CAMERAS

The quest for a small, unobtrusive camera to take smaller-than-usual pictures started in the last century, but it was not until the 1880s that a steady stream of such cameras started to appear on the market, initially for plates and then for rollfilm.

The first miniature camera to take rollfilm was patented in America in 1892 by William V. Esmond. Called the Kombi, it was manufactured in Chicago and took twenty-five 38mm (1.5 inch) pictures on a rollfilm specially manufactured by Eastman Kodak. It took the form of a small, metal box camera made entirely of brass, with an interesting pattern oxidized on to the outside.

A popular camera designed to look like a pocket watch was made under licence in both America and England from about 1905. Designed by the Swedish engineer Magnus Niéll, it was made by the Expo Camera Company of New York under the name 'Watch Camera" and by Houghton's of London under the more colourful name of 'Ticka". It took twenty-five pictures of just 16 x 22mm (⅝ x ⅞ inches).

The minute, bakelite Midget was made by Coronet in Birmingham, England, in the mid-1930s. Five different colours were made and are sought after by collectors, especially as a

CAMERA : Midget
MANUFACTURER : Coronet Camera Co.
DATE : c1935
COUNTRY OF ORIGIN : UK

CAMERA : Kombi
MANUFACTURER : Alfred C. Kemper
DATE : 1892
COUNTRY OF ORIGIN : USA

CAMERA : Stecky model IIIA
MANUFACTURER : Riken Optical
DATE : c1950-1955
COUNTRY OF ORIGIN : Japan

CAMERA : Ticka
MANUFACTURER : G. Houghton & Son
DATE : c1905-1914
COUNTRY OF ORIGIN : UK

complete set. Also in the 1930s one of the most famous sub-miniature cameras appeared. The Minox was made in Latvia and took pictures of 8 x 11mm (0.3 x 0.4 inches) on special film cassettes. After the war, production continued in Germany and several new models were introduced. In 1988, they celebrated 50 years of production with a special gold-plated Minox LX made in limited numbers.

Two notable Japanese sub-miniature cameras came out after the Second World War. The first,

called the Steky, was made in several models between 1947 and the mid-1950s, and became one of the most popular sub-miniature cameras to be sold in the United States. Hence it is rarer, and more expensive, on the European collectors' markets. The second, the Konan-16, appeared in 1950, and introduced a new 16mm cassette which was to become very popular for cameras of this size. Made by Chiyoda Kogaku (who changed their name to Minolta in 1962) it heralded a succession of Minolta 16mm cameras.

CAMERA : Konan-16
MANUFACTURER : Chiyoda Kogaku (Minolta)
DATE : 1950-1957
COUNTRY OF ORIGIN : Japan

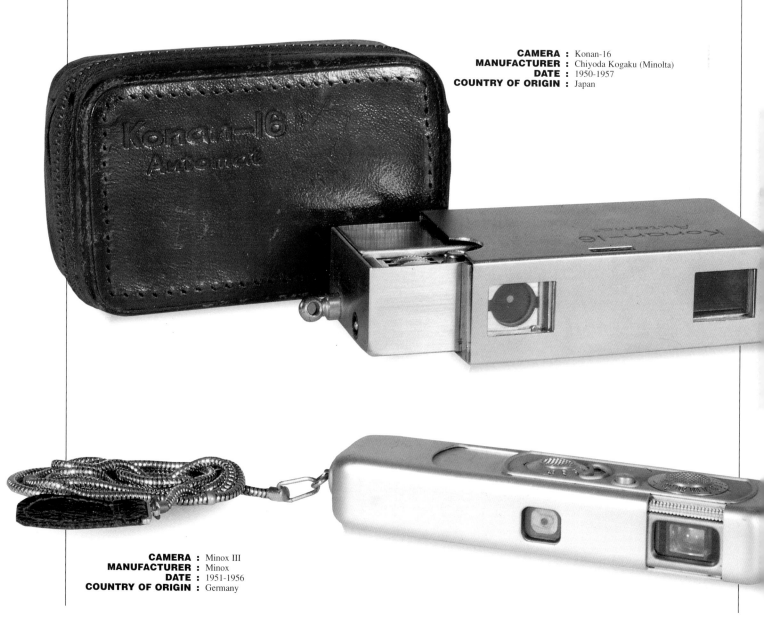

CAMERA : Minox III
MANUFACTURER : Minox
DATE : 1951-1956
COUNTRY OF ORIGIN : Germany

STEREOSCOPIC CAMERAS

Since our eyes are a small distance apart, they see the world from slightly different viewpoints, and it is this phenomenon which the brain uses to interpret the world in three dimensions. Likewise, if two photographs are taken from slightly differing viewpoints and viewed in such a way that each eye sees just one photograph, the brain 'sees' a three-dimensional image. This type of photography is called stereoscopic photography and examples date from as early as 1841.

Throughout the last century, when stereoscopic photography was very popular, various designs of cameras and special viewers were made. One of the best designs to emerge had two side-by-side lenses and a special shutter which would take the

CAMERA : Stereo Weno
MANUFACTURER : Blair Camera Co.
DATE : 1902-1903
COUNTRY OF ORIGIN : USA

exposure simultaneously through each lens. Jules Richard of Paris, France, specialized in manufacturing stereoscopic cameras. His Glyphoscope of 1905 was one of his simpler designs and took 45 x 107mm (1.8 x 4.2 inch) plates. When not in use, the camera could be turned into a viewer for the pictures by looking through it backwards - the front panel was removed so that one could see through the lenses to the slides, which were held at the back.

Contemporary with the Glyphoscope were several cheap stereo rollfilm cameras aimed at the mass market. Among these was the Stereo Weno made in the United States under the name of the Blair Camera Company (although they had just been bought out by Eastman Kodak). It was a simple folding camera which took 8.9cm (3½ inch) square pictures.

CAMERA :	Glyphoscope
MANUFACTURER :	Jules Richard
DATE :	1905
COUNTRY OF ORIGIN :	France

CAMERA :	Stereo Graphic
MANUFACTURER :	Graflex Inc.
DATE :	c1956
COUNTRY OF ORIGIN :	USA

Interest in stereoscopic photography declined until after the Second World War, when several new cameras appeared. The Stereo Realist, marketed from 1947 onwards, used 35mm film and was the most popular post-war stereoscopic camera. Another American 35mm camera of this type was the Stereo Graphic produced by Graflex Inc. from around 1956 onwards. A version of this camera was made under licence by the British manufacturer Wray, but with different lenses.

A recent stereo camera was announced by Nimslo in 1980, although it was not marketed for a further three years. It had an unusual design, with four lenses taking pictures simultaneously on 35mm film. The exposed film was sent back to Nimslo for processing and printing by a special technique, to yield a stereoscopic effect.

CAMERA : Stereo Realist
MANUFACTURER : David White Co.
DATE : 1947
COUNTRY OF ORIGIN : USA

CAMERA : Nimslo 3D
MANUFACTURER : Nimslo Ltd.
DATE : c1983
COUNTRY OF ORIGIN : UK

PANORAMIC CAMERAS

We have all pointed our cameras at a spectacular view, only to be disappointed at the result. A conventional camera cannot record a wide subject such as a large group of people or a broad landscape. To overcome this problem, the panoramic camera is designed to capture a wider angle of view, up to a full 360⁻.

Although there was an interest in panoramic work from the earliest beginnings of photography, it was not until 1896 that the first camera to be widely sold was patented. It was the Al Vista, made in Wisconsin by the Multiscope & Film Company, and several models were manufactured up to 1908. It had one of the standard panoramic camera designs in which the lens rotated as the exposure was made. The image was recorded on a length of rollfilm which had to be held in a curved plane so that each part of the film lay the same distance from the lens. The same basic design was used by the Kodak Panoram cameras which were made from 1899-1928.

An alternative to having the lens rotate was simply to use a very wide angle lens. The first such camera was patented in England by Thomas Sutton in 1859 and used a remarkable lens made of a hollow glass sphere filled with water. During the early years of this century, Al Vistas and Kodak Panorams cornered the market, but from the 1930s onwards the wide-angle design had something of a revival. Among the cameras of this period was the Envoy Wide Angle of 1949 which was made in Birmingham, England. Although designed for rollfilm, it could take a plate back, and its lens was capable of recording an angle of 82⁻ (which is approximately equivalent to a 24mm lens on a modern 35mm camera).

As 35mm became popular, a few panoramic cameras appeared for this film size. Among them was the Russian made Horizont (c1966) which was of the rotating lens design. As with many other Russian cameras, the first two digits of the body serial number give the year of manufacture, so dating one of these cameras is easy.

CAMERA : Al Vista
MANUFACTURER : Multiscope & Film Co.
DATE : 1896-1908
COUNTRY OF ORIGIN : USA

CAMERA : No. 4 Kodak Panoram
MANUFACTURER : Eastman Kodak
DATE : 1899-1924
COUNTRY OF ORIGIN : USA

CAMERA : Envoy Wide Angle
MANUFACTURER : Ensigh (Houghtons)
DATE : 1949
COUNTRY OF ORIGIN : UK

CAMERA : Horizont
MANUFACTURER : Krasnogorsk
DATE : c1966
COUNTRY OF ORIGIN : Russia

Appendix

FURTHER READING

McKeown's Price Guide to Antique and Classic Camerasedited by James M. McKeown and Joan C. McKeown. Published biennially by Centennial Photo, Grantsburg, WI 54840, USA.

(The most comprehensive price guide available covering over 8000 cameras. Prices in US dollars but with a good indication of international markets where these differ from the US. Useful for dating and identifying unknown cameras as well.)

Le Foto Saga - The Camera Collector's New Handbook

by Patrice-Hervé Pont (2nd Ed., 1991). Published by Fotosaga, Flassy 58420, Neuilly, France.
(A bilingual (French/English) pocket guide covering where to buy old cameras, addresses of collectors' clubs, books, magazines and much more. Over 1500 useful addresses are listed from nearly forty countries worldwide.)

A History of the 35mm Still Camera

by Roger Hicks. Published by Focal Press, London and Boston, 1984.
(A comprehensive history of 35mm cameras from 1912-1967.)
Kodak Cameras - The First Hundred Years
by Brian Coe. Published in English by Hove Foto Books, 1988; and in German by Callwey.
(Lists every Kodak camera made up to the 1980s, with well-researched details and copious illustrations.)

Hove Foto Books Collectors' Guides

(A series of books giving in-depth coverage of individual manufacturers and their cameras.)

COLLECTORS' CLUBS AND SOCIETIES

Australia
The Photographic Collectors Society, c/o Ted Bedgood, 14 Warne Street, Eaglemont, VIC 3084
Camera Collectors Society of Western Australia, PO Box 29, Kelmscott, W A 6111
Canada
The Photographic Historical Society of Canada, PO Box 115, Postal Station 'S', Toronto, Ontario M5M 4L6
Western Canada Photographic Historical Association, PO Box 33742, Vancouver, BC V6J 4L6
Japan
All Japan Classic Camera Club, c/o Monarch Mansion Kohrakuen, Room 802, 24-11, 2-chome Kasuga, Bunkyo-ku, Tokyo 112
UK
Photographic Collectors Club of Great Britain, 5 Station Industrial Estate, Low Prudhoe, Northumberland, NE42 6NP
USA
American Society of Camera Collectors, 4918 Alcove Avenue, North Hollywood, CA 91607
American Photographic Historical Society, c/o George Gilbert, 520 West 44th Street, New York, NY 10036
Western Photographic Collectors Association, PO Box 4294, Whittier, CA 90607

INDEX